HOW TO DRAW YOUR OWN GRAPHIC NOVEL

TELLING THE STORY IN YOUR GRAPHIC NOVEL

CHILDREN'S LIBRARY   FRANK LEE

PowerKiDS
press™
New York

Published in 2012 by The Rosen Publishing Group, Inc.

29 East 21st Street, New York, NY 10010

Copyright © 2012 Arcturus Publishing Limited

Text and Illustrations: Frank Lee with Jim Hansen and Peter Gray

Editors: Joe Harris and Kate Overy

U.S. Editor: Kara Murray

Design: Andrew Easton

Cover Design: Andrew Easton

Library of Congress Cataloging-in-Publication Data

Lee, Frank, 1980—

Telling the story in your graphic novel / by Frank Lee.

    p. cm. —— (How to draw your own graphic novel)

Includes index.

 ISBN 978-1-4488-6434-8 (library binding) —— ISBN 978-1-4488-6453-9 (pbk.) ——

ISBN 978-1-4488-6454-6 (6-pack)

1. Comic books, strips, etc.——Authorship——Juvenile literature. 2. Comic books, strips, etc.——Illustrations——Juvenile literature. 3. Graphic novels——Authorship——Juvenile literature. 4. Cartooning——Technique——Juvenile literature. I. Title.

PN6710.L42 2012

741.5′1——dc23

                                                2011030627

Printed in China

SL002072US

CPSIA Compliance Information: Batch #AW2102PK: For Further Information contact Rosen Publishing, New York, New York at 1-800-237-9932

CONTENTS

DRAWING TOOLS

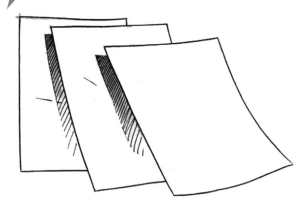

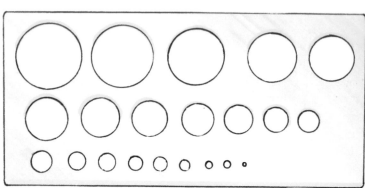

CIRCLE TEMPLATE
This is very useful for drawing small circles.

LAYOUT PAPER
Most professional illustrators use cheaper paper for basic layouts and practice sketches before they get around to the more serious task of producing a masterpiece on more costly paper. It's a good idea to buy some plain paper from a stationery shop for all of your practice sketches. Go for the least expensive kind.

DRAWING PAPER
This is a heavy-duty, high-quality paper, ideal for your final version. You don't have to buy the most expensive brand. Most decent art or craft shops stock their own brand or a student brand and, unless you're thinking of turning professional, these will do fine.

WATERCOLOR PAPER
This paper is made from 100 percent cotton and is much higher quality than wood-based papers. Most art shops stock a large range of weights and sizes. Paper that is 140 pounds (300 g/m) should be fine.

FRENCH CURVES
These are available in a few shapes and sizes and are useful for drawing curves.

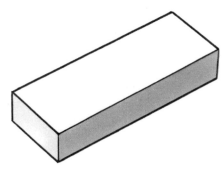

ERASER
There are three main types of eraser: rubber, plastic, and putty. Try all three to see which kind you prefer.

PENCILS

It's best not to cut corners on quality here. Get a good range of graphite (lead) pencils ranging from soft (#1) to hard (#4).

Hard lead lasts longer and leaves less graphite on the paper. Soft lead leaves more lead on the paper and wears down more quickly. Every artist has their personal preference, but #3 pencils are a good medium range to start out with until you find your favorite.

Spend some time drawing with each weight of pencil and get used to their different qualities. Another good product to try is the mechanical pencil. These are available in a range of lead thicknesses, 0.5 mm being a good medium range. These pencils are very good for fine detail work.

PENS

There is a large range of good-quality pens on the market these days and all will do a decent job of inking. It's important to experiment with different pens to determine which you are most comfortable using.

You may find that you end up using a combination of pens to produce your finished artwork. Remember to use a pen that has waterproof ink if you want to color your illustration with a watercolor or ink wash. It's a good idea to use one of these anyway. There's nothing worse than having your nicely inked drawing ruined by an accidental drop of water!

BRUSHES

Some artists like to use a fine brush for inking linework. This takes a bit more practice and patience to master, but the results can be very satisfying. If you want to try your hand at brushwork, you will definitely need to get some good-quality sable brushes.

MARKERS

These are very versatile pens and, with practice, can give pleasing results.

INKS

With the dawn of computers and digital illustration, materials such as inks have become a bit obscure, so you may have to look harder for these. Most good art and craft shops should stock them, though.

THE ELEMENTS OF A PAGE

There are two main types of comic book page. A splash page is designed for maximum impact and showcases a single image. This gives the artist a good opportunity to show off! A standard page is made up of several smaller images, or panels, and moves the story along.

SPLASH PAGE

Comic books sometimes begin with a splash page, which draws the reader into the story. They can also be used to give extra punch to the most dramatic moments in a story, such as when the mysterious villain reveals his true identity or the hero falls from a cliff edge.

A splash page has to be attention grabbing. In this example, heavy shadow and an unusual point of view have been used to create atmosphere.

Narrative captions can be used to tell the story or to reveal a character's thoughts. However, you should never give the same information in the picture and text.

DEX LARROCA WAS RUNNING OUT OF TIME. IF HE WAS TO BUST THIS CASE WIDE OPEN, HE'D HAVE TO RESORT TO THE TOUGHEST KIND OF CRIME INVESTIGATION—THE HARD-BOILED KIND!

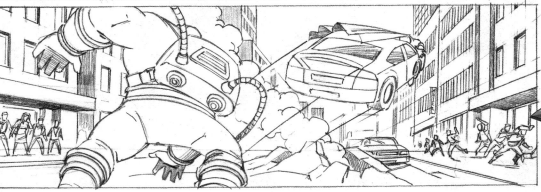

STANDARD PAGE
This is the most common type of comic book page.

A single illustration is called a panel.

When you see type like "Brunkle," it is, of course, a sound effect.

The space between the panels is called the gutter.

Speech bubbles are known as dialogue balloons.

End your comic book page with a dramatic action shot to make it a real page-turner!

PANELS AND COMPOSITION

TYPES OF PANELS

In many ways, planning a comic book is similar to making a movie. A movie director chooses the position from which her camera will get the most effective shot. As a comic book artist, it's up to you to find the angles that will illustrate the plot clearly, while keeping the reader interested.

The panel below is called a medium shot. The action is viewed from fairly nearby, and the reader can see the figures from head to toe.

FREEZE!

This panel (above) is called a close-up. This is where you zoom in very closely on the action. Close-ups are often used to focus on a character's facial expressions and emotions.

This panel is called a long shot or a panoramic shot. It is used when the story requires a wide-angle shot to show the setting, rather than focusing on the characters.

Here is another long shot, but this time the action is seen from above, as a bird's-eye view.

This angle is called a worm's-eye view. It shows the action from below.

Here, the main details are shown in solid black. This is called a silhouette.

PANELS IN STORYTELLING

How will your choice of panel types affect the story? Composition, or layout, is a very important part of comic book art. Each panel must be carefully composed so that the story is easy to follow. The action should flow from panel to panel in a way that is eye-catching, too.

SETTING THE SCENE

This long shot has been chosen to set up the story. It leaves the reader eager to discover what will happen next.

A Western reader will normally scan a page from left to right and top to bottom. Notice how the elements in this panel flow from left to right. This is the order in which they will be viewed.

PACKING IN INFORMATION

This wide-angle shot is bursting with action and information. All the elements work logically so that the reader can immediately understand the story. A comic book page should be drawn so that it all makes sense without the aid of captions or dialogue balloons.

FRAMING THE ACTION
Here is a close-up shot. It's an intense scene in which the hero is rushing to save a woman who is trapped in a burning building. Notice how the main interest is grouped in the top half of the frame. The smoke, below, is used to frame the action.

DRAMATIC SHAPES
Here is another wide shot. Notice how the position of the woman's body forms a triangle. The forest makes a curve around her.

TELLING A SUPERHERO STORY

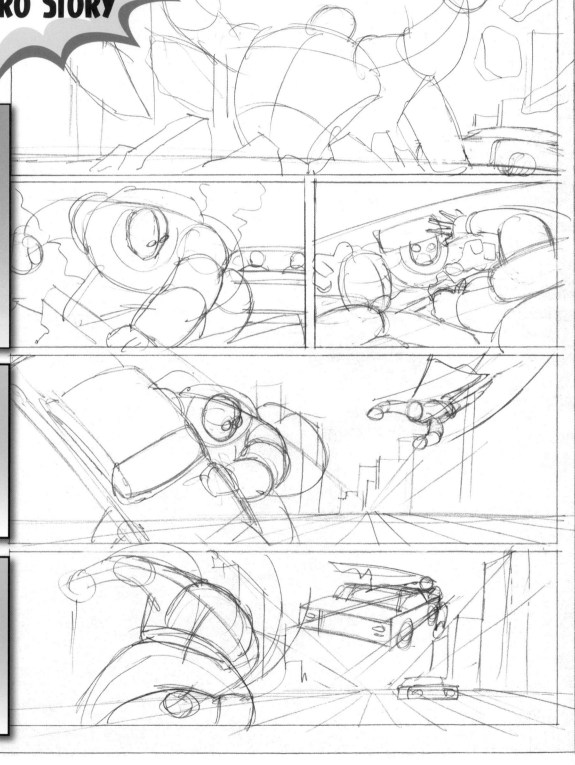

OMEGAMAN VS THE ANNIHILATOR

THE PLOT

A huge monster is rampaging through the center of a big city. The creature lifts a car, terrifying its passengers. Just at this moment, our hero, Omegaman, arrives at the scene. The monster attacks!

STEP 1: FIRST DRAFT

A first draft is all about figuring out how the action will flow from panel to panel. The figures are drawn very roughly, first in stick figure form then with simple construction shapes.

PERSPECTIVE

Draw perspective lines so you get the angle of the buildings right, and sketch a rough grid to help you scale the foreground and background objects correctly in relation to one another.

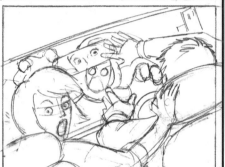

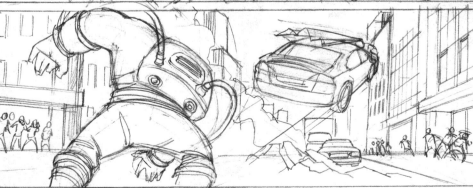

STEP 2:
ADDING DETAIL
Start to flesh out your figures and add detail. This page is packed with action, so keep your figures looking dynamic.

BUILDINGS
Using the perspective lines that you drew at the first draft stage, map out the shapes of the buildings and their various heights. Take care to draw the windows of each building accurately.

CARS
Base the cars on real vehicles. You could look at some parked cars in your street or neighborhood and do some sketches. If you base your content on real objects and pay attention to detail, your drawings will look much more realistic and polished.

TAKE YOUR TIME
Don't rush! The more time you spend getting all the little details right at this stage, the more believable your final page will look.

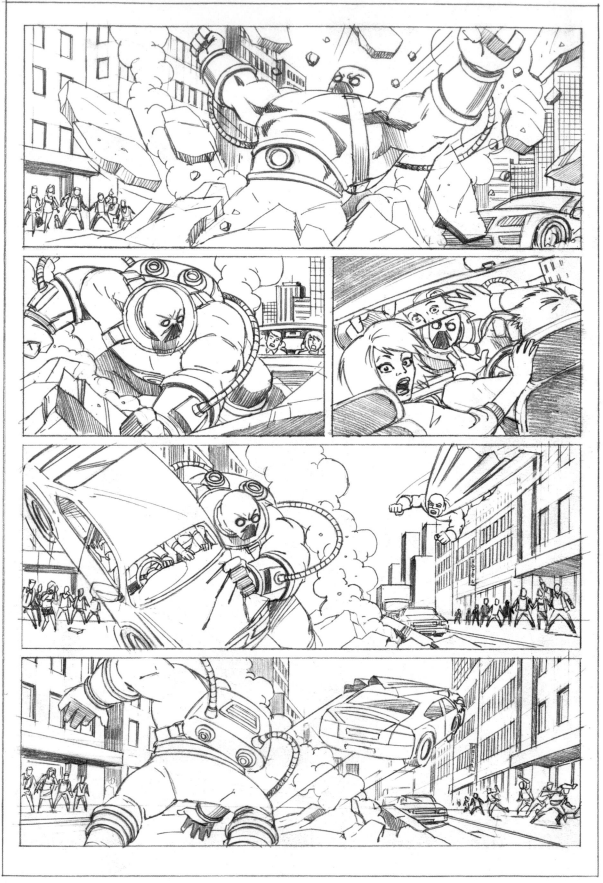

STEP 3: THE FINAL PENCILED PAGE

Look at the finished comic book page opposite. As you can see, we haven't included any text in this pencil page. This is to demonstrate how, when drawn correctly, a series of panels can clearly tell a story without any dialogue. The guide below gives a description of each panel.

PANEL 1
This shows the entrance of the crazy monster as it smashes up through the road, scattering debris everywhere. We also see a car screeching to a halt on the far right. This is the reader's first sight of the monster's victims.

PANEL 2
Next, the monster climbs out of the hole in the ground and notices the car and its passengers.

PANEL 3
We now switch to a point of view inside the car, as the monster approaches and grabs the hood.

PANEL 4
A wide shot shows both the monster and the hero rushing to the rescue. The monster turns its back away from the hero, holding the car like a weapon...

PANEL 5
The monster hurls the car with the passengers still inside at Omegaman. But what happens next?

STEP 4: INKING
Take time to carefully ink over the pencil drawing.

INKING TOOLS
A technical inking pen has been used for the straight lines. A brush ink pen has been used for the linework in the foreground.

TYPES OF LINES
Different lines widths can make objects look distant or close. Use light, thin linework for objects in the background. Use bolder linework for the objects in the foreground so that they stand out. This will make the drawing look less flat.

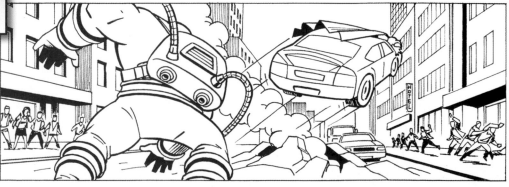

STEP 5: COLORING
This scene is set in daytime, so a pale blue sky has been used in all panels. The buildings are a mixture of off-white, sand, beige, and pale grays. A cool gray has been used for the road and scarlet for the car.

SINISTER SHADES
The villain's costume has been colored using a light blue overlayed with gray. The metallic parts of the suit have been colored cadmium yellow. A cool gray has been chosen for the boots.

HEROIC HUES
The colors we have chosen for the superhero are sky blue for the mask and cape and pale blue for the body.

TELLING A CRIME STORY

THE LARROCA AFFAIR

THE PLOT:
Hard-boiled cop Dex Larroca is hoping to arrest a dangerous criminal. He follows a lead to an abandoned warehouse and breaks in to search the building.

STEP 1: FIRST DRAFT
Rough out the story in the panels using simple shapes to establish the composition and content of each one.

Consider the different types of panels and which angle will work best for each step of the action. Remember to keep it simple but exciting!

Stop every so often and take a look at the whole page. Ensure the story makes sense from panel to panel before you add any detail.

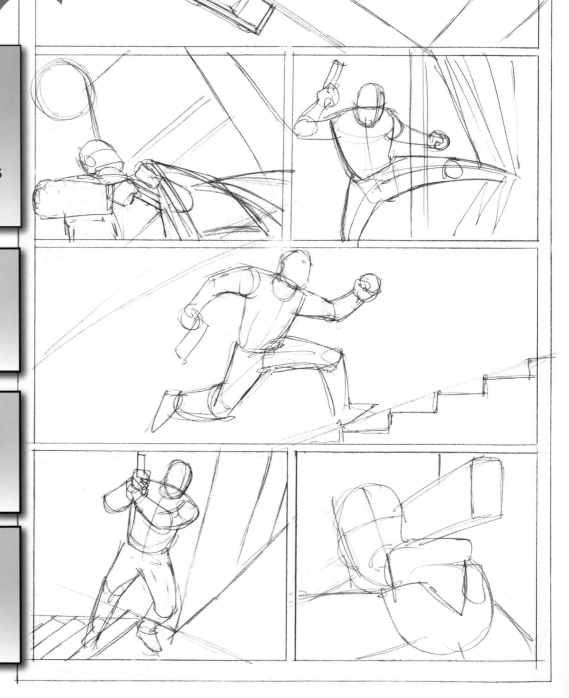

STEP 2: ADDING DETAIL

Once you are happy that the series of panels works effectively, start to add more detail to your layout.

ON THE GRID

Use grid lines to help get the perspective correct. As there need to be lots of different viewpoints and angles from panel to panel, you need to be careful to get the perspective just right on each one. Grids are also useful for accurately plotting where the windows of buildings should go.

CONSISTENCY

Try to keep the look of your character consistent from panel to panel. Do lots of sketches before you start your comic book page, so you know every detail of your character's appearance.

STEP 3: THE FINAL PENCILED PAGE

On the page opposite you can see Dex Larroca in action in the finished comic book page. See how shading and fine details have been added, such as the timberwork on the boarded-up windows and exposed brickwork where plaster has broken away. The final panel of the story leaves the reader guessing who or what might be waiting for Dex as he turns the corner.

PANEL 1
We open with a bird's-eye view of Dex pulling up outside the warehouse. This angle is excellent for establishing a location. It also makes the reader feel that the character is being watched.

PANEL 2
Here we have a worm's-eye view as Dex gets ready to enter the building.

PANEL 3
This is a straight-on medium shot.

PANEL 4
This is a kind of wide-angle medium shot. It gives a strong sense of sideways movement.

PANEL 5
Again, this angle suggests that Dex may be being secretly observed by someone outside the panel. This creates extra suspense and a feeling of unease in the reader.

PANEL 6
Finally, we cut to an intense close-up as Dex turns the corner. He shouts, "FREEZE!"

STEP 4: INKING
Trace over your pencil lines, again using stronger, thicker lines for the objects in the foreground.

CRIME NOIR
Notice how some areas are filled with solid black. For example the sides of buildings, the stairs, and Dex's legs and feet are filled with ink. This is not strictly realistic, but it gives a nice sense of weight and contrast to a comic book page. Heavy use of solid ink blocks is especially popular in crime and horror comics.

STEP 5: COLORING

A different color palette is used in the first three and second three panels. This gives a different feeling to the outdoor and indoor scenes.

OUTDOOR COLORS

A base color of pale blue was applied to panels 1, 2, and 3 so that when other colors were added over the top it would give a moonlight tone to the scene.

INDOOR COLORS

Panels 4, 5, and 6 are inside the building. Dark tones of gray were used to give the place a gritty, poorly lit feel. A very pale gray was also used as a base for the detective.

FREEZE!

TELLING A SCIENCE FICTION STORY

SPACE APE ATTACK!

THE PLOT:
Space pilots Zak and Lara return to their satellite headquarters to find that it has been infested by aliens. And not just any aliens, but the most dangerous kind of all: man-eating space apes!

STEP 1: FIRST LAYOUT
It's a good idea to experiment with different layouts. Your page must be dynamic and exciting but also easy to read.

WHAT'S WRONG HERE?
The panels in this layout are all roughly the same size, which gives us very little space for the action. The characters are more or less viewed from the same angle and distance throughout. The layout could be much more dynamic and varied, and the final panel would work better with more room to breathe.

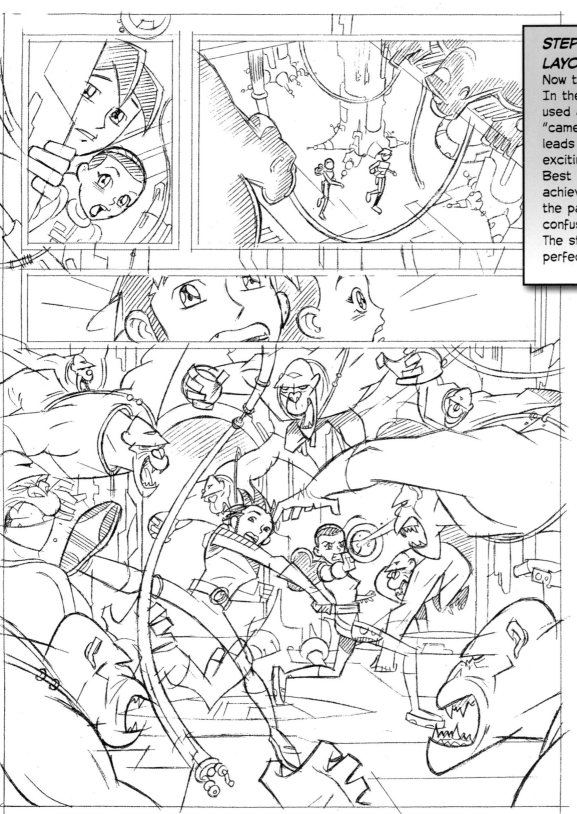

STEP 2: REVISED LAYOUT

Now this is much better. In these layouts we've used a range of different "camera" angles. Everything leads up to the final exciting action panel. Best of all, this has been achieved without making the panel sizes and angles confusing or distracting. The story still makes perfect sense.

STEP 3: INKING
This page has been inked with sharp, neat lines. Heavier lines are used for the outlines of objects. The edges of the panels have been given a very thick, stylized line. Notice how the gutters of the first three images are part of the large image below.

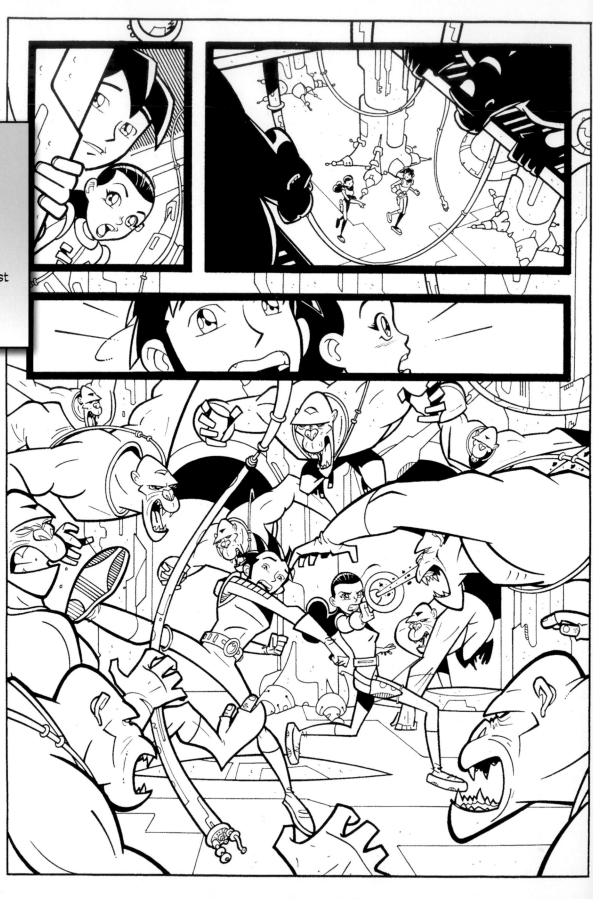

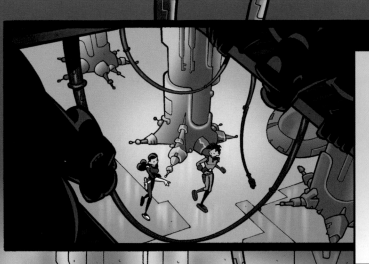

STEP 4: COLORING
Here's the finished page. The main palette that we have chosen for this page is a mixture of purple and gray. Zak and Lara stand out against this background because of their contrasting red and blue costume colors.

COMPUTER COLORS
Unlike the previous colored pages, which were colored in a traditional way, this page has been colored using a computer. The inked artwork was scanned into the computer, and the program Photoshop was used for coloring.

EXPRESSIONS IN STORYTELLING

FACE TO FACE
The best comic book storytellers are masters of facial expressions. These will communicate your characters' feelings, motivations, and personalities. The best way to practice expressions is to use a mirror or ask a volunteer (a family member or friend perhaps) to model for you.

This superhero's smile is friendly, relaxed, and confident. He looks trustworthy and carefree.

This cop's expression is angry but determined. Unlike the superhero, he looks as if he is carrying the weight of the world on his shoulders.

There are as many facial expressions as there are emotions! Here are some common ones for you to practice.

Downbeat

Gloating

Determined

In love

Enraged

Scornful

GLOSSARY

captions (CAP-shunz) Text set within the panels of a graphic novel. The captions work with the pictures to tell the story.

composition (kom-puh-ZIH-shun) How the elements of an artwork or a comic book page are arranged to make them look appealing.

construction shapes (kun-STRUK-shun SHAYPS) Shapes, such as blocks and balls, that are drawn over a sticklike figure to make it more three-dimensional.

dialogue balloons (DY-uh-lawg BUH-loonz) Oval shapes that contain text representing speech. A pointing element links the text to the speaker.

layout (LAY-owt) A sketch that shows where items, such as panels, pictures, and captions, will be positioned on each page.

page-turner (PAYJ-tur-ner) A dramatic work that makes the reader want to turn the page to see what happens next.

perspective (per-SPEK-tiv) A way of drawing items so that they look correctly sized and shaped in relation to each other and in relation to the point from which they are being viewed.

plot (PLOT) The series of events that make up a story.

point of view (POYNT UV VYOO) The direction and angle from which the reader or artist is viewing the objects and people in a picture, such as from above or below.

science fiction (SY-unts FIK-shun) Stories set in a future world.

stick figure (STIK FIH-gyur) A simple drawing of a figure using lines and circles.

FURTHER READING

Besel, Jennifer M. *The Captivating, Creative, Unusual History of Comic Books.* Unusual Histories. Mankato, MN: Capstone Press, 2010.

Carson Levine, Gail. *Writing Magic: Creating Stories That Fly.* New York: Collins, 2006

Kistler, Mark. *Dare to Draw in 3-D.* Learn to Draw. New York: Scholastic, 2003.

Rosinsky, Natalie M. *Write Your Own Graphic Novel.* Mankato, MN: Compass Point Books, 2008.

Slate, Barbara. *You Can Do a Graphic Novel.* New York: Alpha Books, 2010.

Templeton, Ty, Ron Boyd, John Delaney, and Walter Foster. *How to Draw Batman and the DC Comics Super Heroes.* Irvine, CA: Walter Foster Publishing, 2000.

WEB SITES

Due to the changing nature of Internet links, PowerKids Press has developed an online list of Web sites related to the subject of this book. This site is updated regularly. Please use this link to access the list:

www.powerkidslinks.com/hdgn/story/

INDEX